GLORY

GLORY

Written by
Nancy White Carlstrom

Illustrated by
Debra Reid Jenkins

EERDMANS BOOKS FOR YOUNG READERS

Grand Rapids, Michigan / Cambridge, U.K.

For Mary and Andy, Sarah, Hannah, and Leah Ekblad
with love. — N. W. C.

Dedicated in loving memory to my mother, Peggy Reid,
who taught me to see the glory in all things large and small.
— D. R. J.

Published 2001 by Eerdmans Books for Young Readers
An imprint of Wm. B. Eerdmans Publishing Company
255 Jefferson S.E., Grand Rapids, Michigan 49503
P.O. Box 163, Cambridge CB3 9PU U.K.

Library of Congress-in-Publication Data
Carlstrom, Nancy White.
Glory / written by Nancy White Carlstrom;
illustrated by Debra Reid Jenkins.
p. cm.
Summary: A poem which call upon all creatures to give glory
and praise to the Creator.
ISBN 0-8028-5143-6 (cloth: alk. paper)
1. Children's poetry, American. 2. Creation — Juvenile poetry.
[1. Creation — Poetry. 2. American poetry.]
I. Jenkins, Debra Reid ill. II. Title.
PS 3553.A7355 G57 2001
811'.54 — dc21

The illustrations were painted in oils on canvas.
The display type was set in Carleton.
The text type was set in Zapf Calligraphic 801.
Glory was first presented as a children's liturgy
at First Presbyterian Church in Fairbanks, Alaska.

GLORY be to God for fluttering wings,

for chickadees and butterflies

that dot the skies

like words,

dragonflies and hummingbirds

and all small things

that wing their praise.

GLORY be to God for gills and fins

and all that moves upon the ocean floor,

for coral, sponge, and urchins' spiny points,

quick fish in bold design of every hue

and drabber sorts that dart

or lurk in shadows dim,

for those who praise

in ways they swim.

GLORY be to God for fuzzy spots
of worms and wrigglers,
stripes and polka dots,

the beetle's dance, the spider's poise,

the lizard's leap,

all crickets' joyous noise,

curling bugs and slugs and snails

that whisper holy praise in silver trails.

GLORY be to God for all things wild,

for feral families — mother, father, child.

Through tangled verdant jungle home

with speed and strength and might they roam,

prowling, howling, on and on,

the mighty chorus of the dawn.

A fiercely untamed praise is theirs,

this thundering roar of primal prayers.

GLORY be to God for friendly fur,

for wiggling nose and racing heart,

for twitching ears and throbbing purr,

tails that stretch and tails that wag,

tail buttons soft as cotton.

Their praise is hummed within them deep

or overflows in barking.

And not the least of these

are beasts

who sing to God in silence.

GLORY GLORY GLORY

be to God for winging, swimming, singing ones

of sky and sea and earth.

All creatures large,

all creatures small,

that dance and leap

and curl and crawl,

the wild, the tame —

All creatures by their being

praise their Creator's name.